Contents

More Women in Profile

Explorers

When women began to explore faraway places, they traveled as part of a family. Wife, husband, and children all moved together, looking for somewhere better to live. These explorers traveled because it was necessary. War or **famine** had driven them from their homes.

In later years, some women purposely chose to travel far from home. Many of the earliest women explorers were members of the Christian church. In the eighth century, for instance, English nuns went to Germany to teach Christianity to the people who lived there.

Explorers

on or befo

Carlotta Hacker

Crabtree Publishing Company

Dedication

This series is dedicated to every woman who has followed her dreams and to every young girl who hopes to do the same. While overcoming great odds and often oppression, the remarkable women in this series have triumphed in their fields. Their dedication, hard work, and excellence can serve as an inspiration to all—young and old, male and female. Women in Profile *is both an acknowledgment of and a tribute to these great women.*

Project Manager
Lauri Seidlitz
Crabtree Editor
Virginia Mainprize
Copy Editors
Krista McLuskey
Leslie Strudwick
Design and Layout
Warren Clark

Published by Crabtree Publishing Company

350 Fifth Avenue, Suite 3308
New York, NY
USA 10018

360 York Road, R.R. 4
Niagara-on-the-Lake
Ontario, Canada
L0S 1J0

Cataloging-in-Publication Data

Hacker, Carlotta.
      Explorers / Carlotta Hacker.
          p. cm. — (Women in profile)
      Includes bibliographical references and index.
      Summary: Profiles the lives and accomplishments of such women known for their travels as Isabella Bird Bishop, Amelia Earhart, Mary Kingsley, Annie Smith Peck, Freya Stark, and Valentina Tereshkova.
      ISBN 0-7787-0004-6 (RLB). — ISBN 0-7787-0026-7 (PB)
      1. Women explorers—Biography—Juvenile literature. [1. Women explorers. 2. Explorers. 3. Women—Biography.] I. Title. II Series.
G200.H25 1998   98-10861
910'.82—DC21   CIP
                                      AC

More recently, women have traveled with a different purpose. Like male explorers, they wanted to discover the unknown, to go where no one had been before. They had a great sense of adventure, great courage, and great curiosity.

In the twentieth century, new opportunities for travel have opened up. It is now possible to explore the skies as well as the land and sea. Some of the most daring adventurers have been women. They have traveled in everything from spaceships and airplanes to bicycles and sailboats.

The women you will read about here are just a few of many. They led the way not only for other women, but also for men. They all lived at least part of their lives in the twentieth century. They are among the century's greatest explorers.

You may want to learn more about these women and about other women explorers, too. Use the Suggested Reading list to find books about some of the world's most adventurous women.

"She was seated in the back drawing-room in a big armchair, with gold-embroidered slippers ... and a ribbon and order across her shoulders given to her by the King of the Sandwich Islands."

Marianne North, upon meeting Isabella at a party

Isabella Bird Bishop

English Explorer

Early Years

Isabella was born in the north of England, where her father was a clergyman. As a child, she was made to read the whole Bible—more than a thousand pages. All her relatives were deeply religious. Her mother taught Sunday school, and one of her aunts was a **missionary** in India.

Isabella heard a lot about missionaries when she was growing up in the quiet English countryside. Missionaries went all over the world teaching Christianity. They believed it was their duty to convert others to their religion.

Isabella did not want to be a missionary, but she did want to travel. In 1854, her father gave her £100, which was quite a lot of money in those days, and told her to go wherever she liked. She went to Canada and the United States. While she was away, she wrote long letters to her sister, Henrietta, describing her travels. These letters were published as a book after her return to England. Isabella made other trips in the next few years, but her real travels had not yet begun.

BACKGROUNDER

The Bird Family

Isabella's parents, Edward and Dora Bird, were members of the Clapham Sect, an active religious group. They were relatives of William Wilberforce, the reformer who helped get the slave trade **abolished**. Although the trade was stopped, slavery continued in many areas, especially on sugar and cotton plantations. Because of this slavery, Isabella's aunts would not take sugar in their tea.

Isabella in 1861.

BACKGROUNDER

Traveling the Hard Way

Before the invention of cars and airplanes, travel was slow and uncomfortable. In industrialized countries, there were plenty of trains, but many parts of the world had no railroads. Explorers rode mules, horses, or camels. Often they went on foot. They thought nothing of walking twenty-five miles (forty kilometers) a day. All travel between continents was by ship. Even after there were passenger airlines, most people still chose to cross the Atlantic by ship. Flying did not become popular until the late 1950s.

Developing Skills

Isabella's most exciting travels started in the 1870s after both her parents had died. She was feeling so depressed that she had terrible headaches and backaches. Her doctor said it would do her good to get away for a bit, but he did not expect her to go quite so far. She set off for Australia.

The voyage took almost two months, and Isabella loved every minute. Instead of coming straight home afterwards, she crossed the Pacific Ocean to Hawaii. A bad storm on the way almost sank her ship. Isabella was not scared. She found the rough seas and winds exciting. She had never felt so alive.

In Hawaii, Isabella rode around the islands on horseback. Like many people in those days, she had been riding since she was a child. Horses were the most common form of transportation before cars were invented. In England, women had to ride side-saddle, with both legs on the same side of the horse. This took a good deal of skill and was often uncomfortable. Isabella found that in Hawaii it was not thought unladylike to sit astride a horse the way men did. Afterwards, she always rode astride.

After her trip to Hawaii, Isabella often traveled on horseback, seated astride her animal.

Whenever Isabella went riding, she wore a bloomer costume. This shocked some people. Bloomers were very baggy pants worn under a skirt. In Isabella's day, only men wore pants. Women wore long skirts down to the ground.

Dressed in her bloomers, Isabella explored Hawaii. She rode up the slopes of the volcanoes and peered into their craters. One of them, Mauna Loa, was dangerously active. Smoke and sparks shot out of its crater. Isabella was impressed. She called it "the mightiest volcano in the world."

From Hawaii, Isabella sailed to the United States to see the Rocky Mountains. She explored them with a man called Rocky Mountain Jim. He fell in love with her and asked her to marry him. Isabella said no. She did not approve of his drinking alcohol. Besides, she was looking for an adventure, not a husband.

Quick Notes

- Hawaii was called the Sandwich Islands when Isabella went there.

- Isabella published her first books under the name Isabella Bird. After she married John Bishop, she signed herself Isabella Bird Bishop. John died five years after their marriage.

- Isabella was never fussy about what she ate on her travels. John said she had "the appetite of a tiger and the digestion of an ostrich."

"This is the height of enjoyment in traveling. I have just encamped under a lauhala tree, with my saddle inverted for a pillow, my horse tied by a long lariat to a guava bush."

Isabella always traveled with a lot of equipment, including a large, old-fashioned camera and a revolver. She liked to be prepared for anything.

Accomplishments

Isabella spent most of her life traveling. Between trips, she stayed with her sister in Scotland and wrote books. She wrote nine travel books altogether.

Unlike other women explorers, Isabella was not very interested in the people she met. It was the scenery that thrilled her—and the danger. She never minded being uncomfortable. Nor did she care what she ate.

When Isabella was fifty-eight, she decided to visit Christian missions in India, Turkey, and **Persia**. She later spent three years traveling through Korea, Japan, and China. Sometimes Isabella joined a large group of missionaries. Other journeys were made with just a few local people as guides and helpers.

Isabella's most dangerous journeys were in China. Once, she was surrounded by a crowd of angry Chinese people. Although she was wearing Chinese clothes, she was obviously a **foreigner**.

"I was seated in my chair when it began," Isabella later wrote. "Soon a crowd of men were waving their arms in my face, shouting and yelling." Isabella did not run away. She sat there, staring straight ahead, "never moving a muscle." Her calm reaction probably saved her life.

Despite the danger, Isabella made a long journey through China up the Yangtze River. Isabella was over sixty by this time. When she left the boat to go overland, she rode in a "carrying chair." This was a chair slung on long poles and carried by two men.

The trip took Isabella 900 miles (1,440 kilometers) overland, almost to the border of Tibet. She often stayed in local inns, sleeping in the camp bed she had brought with her. Isabella never stopped traveling. At the age of seventy, she rode 1,000 miles (1,600 kilometers) across Morocco. When she died in England at the age of seventy-three, her trunks were packed for another journey.

"I think that I have contributed so much to the sum of general knowledge of different countries that had I been a man, I should undoubtedly have received some recognition from the Royal Geographic Society."

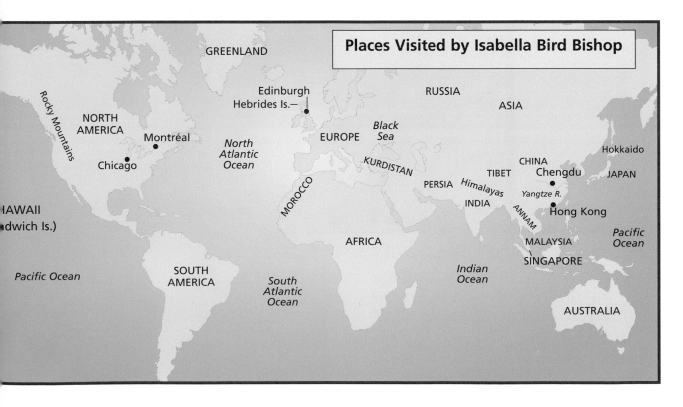

Places Visited by Isabella Bird Bishop

"You will find the unexpected everywhere you go in life. By adventuring about, you become accustomed to the unexpected."

Amelia Earhart

American Pilot

Early Years

"Nothing scares Amelia," her sister, Muriel, used to say. She would watch in awe as Amelia galloped past her on horseback or shot down their homemade roller coaster. Amelia loved the feeling of speed. She and her sister often played outdoors.

The Earharts lived in Kansas City, Missouri, but they often visited Atchison, Kansas, where Amelia had been born. It was her grandmother's home. Later, the family lived in several different cities. Amelia's father, Edwin, worked for the railroad, and he had to live where he could get work. Sometimes he had no job at all. This made things very tough for Amelia's family.

After finishing high school, Amelia enrolled in a school in Pennsylvania, and Muriel went to Canada. By this time, World War I was in full swing. When visiting Muriel in Canada in 1917, Amelia decided to help the war effort. She signed on as a volunteer at a military hospital. There she met men from the **Royal Flying Corps**. She was thrilled by the stories they told. She asked if they would take her up in a plane, but they were not allowed.

BACKGROUNDER

The Early Days of Flying

Airplanes were still very new when Amelia was growing up. The first flight in a "heavier-than-air machine" was made in 1903 by the American brothers Wilbur and Orville Wright. The first seaplane was built in 1911. World War I (1914–18) was the first war in which airplanes were used. After the war, local air shows became very popular. People flocked to see pilots do daring stunts in their tiny planes.

Amelia had the perfect personality for flying. She loved adventure and was unafraid of death.

Developing Skills

"As soon as we left the ground, I knew I myself had to fly.... 'I think I'd like to learn to fly,' I told the family casually that evening."

After the war, Amelia took a course in engine mechanics. That was an unusual subject for a woman to study in those days. However, it was a perfect course for anyone interested in airplanes. Amelia also took a medical course at Columbia University.

By this time, Amelia's parents were living in Los Angeles. She went to an air show there and had a ride in a plane for $10. She was thrilled. It was the most exciting thing she had ever done. Amelia took a job driving a truck so that she could pay for flying lessons. Less than a year later, in June 1921, she made her first **solo** flight. She continued to work hard and save money. On her twenty-fifth birthday, she bought a small plane for $2,000.

Soon after this, Amelia set her first record. She flew higher than any woman had done before—14,000 feet (over 4,000 meters). She also took to barnstorming at air shows, flying upside down and doing other stunts. But Amelia could not make a living this way. She had to have a job, so she became a social worker in Boston. She flew planes in her spare time and became well known as a skilled pilot.

A few years later, some people were looking for a woman to be part of the crew in a plane flying across the Atlantic Ocean. They asked Amelia if she would go. "How could I refuse such a shining adventure?" she said. No woman had ever been across the Atlantic in a plane. On June 17, 1928, Amelia became the first to do so. The flight took twenty hours and forty minutes.

This flight made Amelia famous, even though she had not been the pilot. She was asked to give lectures. She became vice-president of a small airline company, and she wrote a column on flying for *Cosmopolitan* magazine. Then, in 1932, she set a new record. She became the first woman to fly solo across the Atlantic. Amelia now felt she had earned the fame she had gained four years earlier when she had just been a member of the crew.

BACKGROUNDER

The First Women Pilots

Amelia was the most famous of the early women pilots, but she was by no means the first. The Baroness de la Roche was the first woman to fly. She received her pilot's license in 1909. The first American woman to receive a license was Harriet Quimby in 1911. The following year, Harriet became the first woman to fly across the English Channel. In 1920, Bessie Coleman became the first African-American woman to pilot a plane. Bessie was a pilot long before Amelia learned to fly. So was Neta Snook, the pilot who taught Amelia. Neta was the first woman to graduate from the Curtiss School of Aviation.

After giving a talk on air safety to a Senate committee in 1931, Amelia took a new government plane for a test flight.

Accomplishments

During the next few years, Amelia set several new records. In some cases, she was the first woman to do so. In other cases, she was the first person—man or woman. In 1935, Amelia was the first person to fly solo from Hawaii to the United States mainland.

Each time Amelia set a record, she was leading the way for others. She was showing how quick and convenient air travel could become. She wanted to show that it was possible to fly all the way around the world.

Amelia could not do this long flight alone. She had three crew members with her in March 1937 when she took off from Oakland, California, heading west for Hawaii. That first leg of the journey went well, but the airplane crashed when leaving Hawaii. No one was hurt, but the plane had to be sent back to the mainland for repairs.

By the time the plane was mended, two of the crew had dropped out of the venture. As well, the winds and air currents had changed. The best route was flying east. Thus, when Amelia finally began her world flight on June 1, 1937, she left from Miami, Florida. Her only crew member was the navigator, Frederick Noonan.

"The lure of flying is the lure of beauty."

Their first stop was Puerto Rico. From there, they flew to Venezuela and Brazil before crossing the Atlantic to Africa. All went well as Amelia and Frederick made their way east, through Asia and Indonesia to Australia. By the beginning of July, they were in New Guinea, the huge island north of Australia. They had flown 22,000 miles (35,200 kilometers), about three-quarters of the way around the world.

Both Amelia and Frederick knew that the next leg of the journey would be the most difficult. Their destination was Howland Island, 2,500 miles (4,000 kilometers) away. Only 2 miles (3.5 kilometers) long, it is a tiny speck in the middle of the Pacific. They never arrived there. A Coast Guard ship near the island heard a weak radio message from the plane. It said that they were running low on fuel and could not see any land. The Coast Guard tried to get more information but could not make contact. No trace of the plane was ever found.

Quick Notes

- **Amelia was nicknamed Lady Lindy after Charles Lindbergh. In 1927, Lindbergh became the first person to fly solo across the Atlantic Ocean.**

- **One day, Amelia crash-landed in a cabbage patch. She said it did not make her hate flying. It just made her hate cabbages.**

- **Amelia founded the Ninety-Nines, a women's flying club.**

- **Amelia wrote three books about flying. One of her most famous was called *The Fun of It*.**

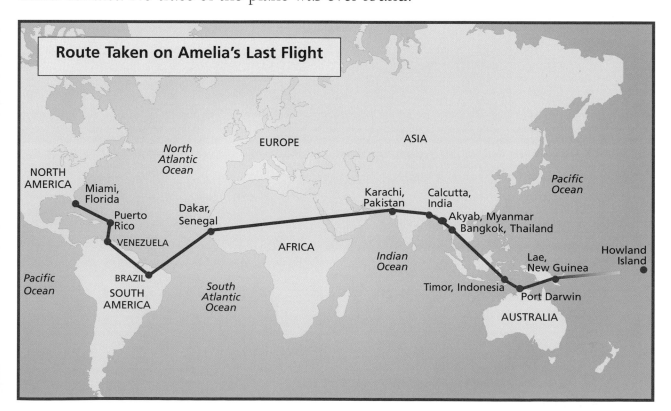

Route Taken on Amelia's Last Flight

"To my taste there is nothing so fascinating as spending a night out in an African forest."

Mary Kingsley

English Explorer in Africa

Early Years

Mary spent the first thirty years of her life in England. Her only journeys were in her imagination, dreaming of the countries her father was visiting. Her father was a traveler who was nearly always far from home.

Mary never went to school, although she did learn to read. Everything she learned was from the books she found in her father's library. Day after day, she pored over them, eager to learn what life was like in the big world outside her home and garden.

Mary's mother was an **invalid** who spent most of her time in bed. Mary rarely left home. Even when she was a small child, she was expected to take care of her mother. She helped with the dusting and cleaning, and did whatever else was needed.

BACKGROUNDER

The Kingsley Family

Mary's uncles were the famous novelists Henry and Charles Kingsley. Her father, George Kingsley, was a doctor by training, but he preferred a life of travel and writing. He did not think women needed an education, so only Mary's brother, Charles, was sent to school. Even so, George liked Mary's help with his research on the places he visited. Mary was eager to do this. She even took German lessons so that she could help her father better.

Mary rarely left her home until she was thirty years old.

BACKGROUNDER

African Exploration

The second half of the nineteenth century is known as the Great Age of African Exploration. It was the time when Dr. Livingstone and other Europeans first traveled deep into the center of the continent. Until then, much of Africa had been "unexplored," although of course the Africans knew the land well. They acted as guides for the European explorers. Despite this, the Europeans claimed the lands as their own. At the Conference of Berlin in 1884, the European countries met together to decide who would own which parts of Africa.

Developing Skills

When Mary was thirty, both her parents died within a few months of each other. Since they had left her a little money, she could afford to travel. There was just one problem. Her brother, Charles, expected her to go on running the house. Mary persuaded him to plan a trip for himself. She then began to plan her own journey.

Mary wanted to go to distant lands, but not to the same ones her father had seen. She dreamed of carrying on his work by exploring places he had not visited. She chose Africa because so little was known about it.

For her first trip, Mary sailed to the Canary Islands. Plenty of ships sailed between there and West Africa, so this seemed a good place to research her trip to Africa. She met many people who had been there and could give her advice.

By the time Mary set out on her second journey, in 1893, she had a good idea what conditions would be like in Africa. She had decided to travel as a trader so that she would meet Africans in a casual way. They would talk to her more easily if she had something to sell. If she just walked around asking questions, they might simply think she was odd.

Mary (front row, center) with a group of other English travelers in Africa in 1895.

Her ship arrived in West Africa in August and gradually worked its way down the coast to the mouth of the Congo River. In the French Congo, just north of the river, Mary journeyed inland, trading as she went. Her only companions were the Africans she hired as her guides. The Europeans on the coast thought her mad to go into the bush. They said she would be murdered.

Mary was not afraid. Wearing a long skirt down to her feet, she marched confidently into the villages. After greeting the people, she showed them her trade goods. She traded fish hooks and other useful gadgets for rubber and ivory. Many of the villagers had never seen a white person. The children were scared and ran away, but their parents gave Mary a warm welcome. They usually offered her their best hut for the night.

By traveling in this way, Mary learned far more than most Europeans. She also realized how much there was to learn about the African culture. She decided to come back on a journey that would take her far from the normal trade routes.

Quick Notes

- **Mary had a great sense of humor and made friends easily.**

- **In the tropical heat of West Africa, Mary wore a long woolen skirt and thick boots. As well, she wore a corset under her blouse. She said, "You have no right to go about Africa in things you would be ashamed to be seen in at home."**

- **West Africa was known as "the white man's grave." This was because so many Europeans died of malaria and other tropical diseases.**

"Every child in the place, as soon as it saw my white face, let a howl out ... and fled to the nearest hut."

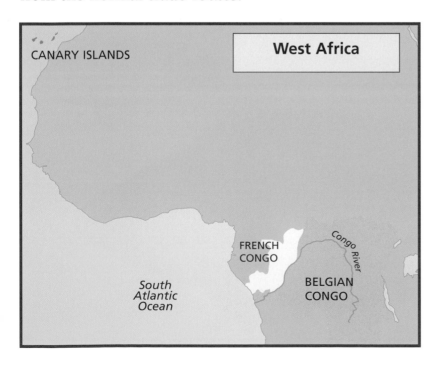

West Africa

CANARY ISLANDS

South Atlantic Ocean

FRENCH CONGO

Congo River

BELGIAN CONGO

Accomplishments

Mary returned to England in June 1894 and was back in the French Congo by December. She remained there for almost a year. This visit was more official than the last one. The Natural History Museum had provided her with collector's equipment so that she could bring back fish and plants. West Africa had many **species** that were unknown in Europe.

Mary was glad to collect for the museum, although her own interest was the people of the region. She came to know them well as she traveled up the Ogooué River. From there she **trekked** through the jungle to the Remboué River which brought her back to the coast. The journey took Mary across country where no white person had been. It also took her into the territory of the Fang people. Mary's guides and helpers were Fangs. They were said to be dangerous, but Mary felt safe with them. She treated them as friends, and they looked after her well.

Mary's detailed sketches and reports added sixty-five new species of fish to scientists' records. Her drawings were published in 1896 in a natural history magazine.

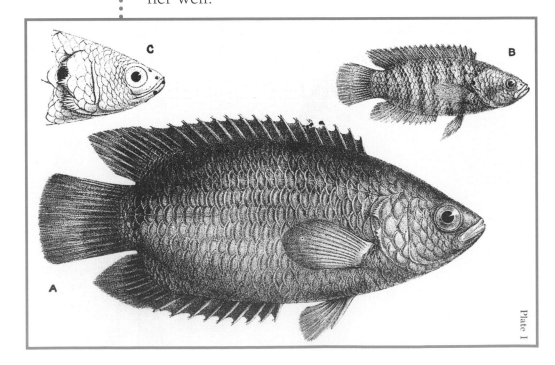

Plate 1

By traveling with the Fangs, Mary learned a great deal about their culture. Eager to share their daily life, she ate whatever was available: palm oil stew, fried fish, and **plantains**. She even ate snake and crocodile. Mary was willing to try anything—even the cures of the medicine men. She offered them her medicines and asked them about their herbs. Everything was of interest to Mary, especially anything to do with African traditions.

When Mary returned to England, she wrote the book *Travels in West Africa*. It was packed with information about the culture of the people. It also told of her adventures—how she had fallen into an elephant trap and tripped over a sleeping leopard. Mary had a **witty** way of writing that made the book very popular.

The lectures Mary gave were not always so popular. She was very outspoken about things she disliked. She especially disliked the way English missionaries were teaching Christianity to the Africans. Mary said that Africans had their own religion. By forbidding them to practice it, the missionaries were destroying African culture. Mary's remarks stirred up a storm.

Mary was planning to return to West Africa, but in 1899, the South African War broke out. This made Mary change her plans. She decided to go to South Africa to nurse the wounded. It was a fatal decision. Mary caught **typhoid fever** from the soldiers she was nursing. She died within days of becoming ill.

BACKGROUNDER

South African War (1899–1902)

Also called the Boer War, the South African War was between Britain and the Dutch settlers in southern Africa. The Dutch settlers were called Boers, or Afrikaners. They had their own Afrikaner **republics** that were separate from the British colonies. After gold was found in Afrikaner territory, many British began to move in. They were not allowed to become citizens, and their gold mines were taxed heavily. Their discontent erupted into a war that was supported by the British government. Britain won the war, and the Afrikaner republics became part of the British Empire.

British soldiers in the trenches fighting the Boers in 1900.

"A firm believer in equality of the sexe I felt that any grea achievement ... wou be an advantage to my sex."

Annie Smith Peck

American Mountain Climber

Early Years

"**G**o away and play with your dolls!" Annie's brothers used to tell her. They would not let her play baseball with them. They said sports were only for boys. This made Annie angry. She had three brothers, and they always left her out of their adventures. Annie decided that one day she would have adventures of her own. She promised herself to do many brave things when she grew up.

Annie and her brothers lived in Providence, Rhode Island. Their father was a lawyer. He and Annie's mother made sure that Annie was given a good education. She went to Providence High School and then trained as a teacher at Rhode Island State Normal School. Annie studied Greek, Latin, and other subjects that her brothers were learning. She was determined to be as good as they were at everything.

After leaving the Normal School, Annie taught school for two terms.

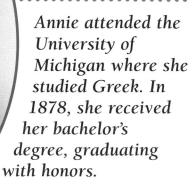

Annie attended the University of Michigan where she studied Greek. In 1878, she received her bachelor's degree, graduating with honors.

Developing Skills

Annie received her master's degree in 1881 and became a full-time teacher. Teaching was one of the few careers a woman could have in the 1880s. She taught Latin, Greek, and math, but she wanted to learn more, so in 1884 she went to Germany to study music. The next year, she traveled to Greece to take a course.

The journey from Germany to Greece changed Annie's life. On her way, she passed the Matterhorn, a famous mountain in the Swiss Alps. Looking up at its massive, snow-covered slopes, Annie longed to climb it. All the great mountaineers had been up the Matterhorn.

Annie had never climbed anything as high as a mountain, but she was soon doing so. Her first attempt was on a small mountain in Europe. She learned a lot on that climb. From then on, each mountain seemed easier. Her first big climb was in 1888, when she reached the top of Mount Shasta in California. In 1895, she stood proudly on the peak of the Matterhorn.

"I wanted to conquer some height where no man had previously explored."

The Matterhorn, on the border between Switzerland and Italy, is 14,692 feet (4,897 meters) high. Snow always covers its peak.

By this time, Annie had given up teaching. She found she could earn a good living by giving lectures. Her climb up the Matterhorn had made her famous. Only two women had ever reached the **summit** before her. People wanted to see Annie and hear of her adventures.

Two years later, Annie climbed Mount Orizaba. At 18,700 feet (5,700 meters), it is the highest mountain in Mexico. Annie was the first woman to reach its summit. Even this did not satisfy her. Being the first woman was not enough. She wanted to be the first person to conquer a high and difficult mountain.

Annie knew that it would be difficult to achieve this goal in Europe. Too many people had already climbed Europe's mountains. In South America, though, there were some mountains that had not been explored.

BACKGROUNDER

Votes for Women

Annie was a **suffragette**. She believed that women should vote in elections. Until 1920, only men were allowed to vote in the United States. When Annie climbed Mount Coropuna in Peru, she planted a flag saying "Votes for Women." Whenever she climbed a mountain, it was to show that a woman could do so. She saw herself as setting an example for other women. She was tougher than many of the men with whom she climbed.

Annie, in 1911, posing with her climbing gear for a photograph.

Annie became an expert on South America and gave many lectures about her travels.

Accomplishments

Annie was more than fifty years old when she climbed Mount Illampu in Bolivia. It is in the Andes mountain range and was thought to be the tallest mountain in South America. In fact, Aconcagua in Argentina is the tallest. It is 22,835 feet (6,960 meters) high. Illampu is 21,300 feet (6,492 meters) high which is still a long and dangerous climb. Annie did not get to the top. An American professor who was climbing with her became ill, and they had to turn back.

Her next challenge was Mount Huascarán in Peru. At 22,205 feet (6,768 meters), it is the second tallest mountain in South America. It had never been climbed, and Annie thought it might be even higher. She thought she could prove it was the highest mountain on the continent.

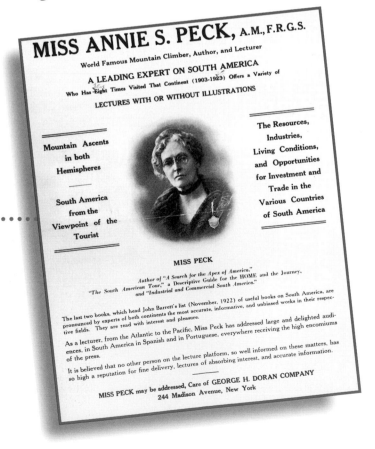

MISS ANNIE S. PECK, A.M., F.R.G.S.

World Famous Mountain Climber, Author, and Lecturer

A LEADING EXPERT ON SOUTH AMERICA

Who Has Eight Times Visited That Continent (1903-1923) Offers a Variety of

LECTURES WITH OR WITHOUT ILLUSTRATIONS

Mountain Ascents in both Hemispheres

South America from the Viewpoint of the Tourist

The Resources, Industries, Living Conditions, and Opportunities for Investment and Trade in the Various Countries of South America

MISS PECK

Author of "A Search for the Apex of America," "The South American Tour," a Descriptive Guide for the HOME and the Journey, and "Industrial and Commercial South America."

The last two books, which head John Barrett's list (November, 1922) of useful books on South America, are pronounced by experts of both continents the most accurate, informative, and unbiased works in their respective fields. They are read with interest and pleasure.

As a lecturer, from the Atlantic to the Pacific, Miss Peck has addressed large and delighted audiences, in South America in Spanish and in Portuguese, everywhere receiving the high encomiums of the press.

It is believed that no other person on the lecture platform, so well informed on these matters, has so high a reputation for fine delivery, lectures of absorbing interest, and accurate information.

MISS PECK may be addressed, Care of GEORGE H. DORAN COMPANY
244 Madison Avenue, New York

She started the climb with a man she had met at the foot of the mountain. When they argued over which route to take, Annie went on alone. It is very dangerous to climb a mountain alone. Climbers usually rope themselves to someone in case they slip. Even so, Annie reached 19,000 feet (5,791 meters) before she had to turn back. Soon afterwards, she tried again by another route. This time she took local guides with her, but again she had to turn back.

By this time, Annie was running short of money. Fortunately, a New York magazine offered her $600 if she would write a story about her climbing. That was a big sum in those days. Annie tried twice more to climb Huascarán. Each time, she failed to reach the summit.

She finally made it in 1908. She had hired two Swiss guides to climb with her. They had a dreadful time. The snow was heavy, and they lost much of their equipment, but at last they were almost at the summit. Annie felt triumphant. She would be the first person—man or woman—to reach the top of this difficult mountain. But then a terrible thing happened. One of the Swiss guides pushed past her and ran to the summit. After her years of effort, she could not claim to be "the first person." She could only claim to be the first woman and the first American to reach the summit.

During the years that followed, Annie climbed many more mountains. She wrote three books about her experiences and was one of the founders of the American Alpine Club. She climbed her last mountain when she was eighty-two years old.

Quick Notes

- In 1927, the north peak of Mount Huascarán was named *Cumbre Aña Peck* in Annie's honor.

- Annie received many awards for her mountaineering. The government of Peru gave her a gold medal, and the Lima Geographical Society gave her a silver slipper.

At the age of seventy-nine, Annie planned to fly in a plane over many of the mountains she had climbed.

*"The lure of exploration continues to be one of the **lodestars** of the human spirit."*

Freya Stark

English Explorer

Early Years

Freya began her travels soon after her birth in Paris, France. Her family moved to Devonshire in England before she was a year old. Soon after that, her family moved again. "My earliest childhood is filled with memories of railway stations," Freya wrote later. Her parents had a big house in Devonshire, but the family was often away traveling through Europe.

Freya's mother, Flora, had been raised in Italy. She was a painter and a pianist. Freya's father, Robert, was an English painter and sculptor. As time passed, Flora and Robert began to live apart. Freya's father stayed in England, and her mother stayed in Italy. Freya and her sister, Vera, lived in both places, but mostly with their mother in Asolo, a town near Venice.

Because of all her family's moving, Freya's education was very hit-and-miss. Sometimes she was taught by a governess. Sometimes she went to school. Always, she was encouraged to read. By the time Freya was nineteen, she had a wide general knowledge and could speak French, German, and Italian.

BACKGROUNDER

A Childhood Accident

When Freya was twelve, she had a terrible accident. Her mother and a friend had a factory that made carpets. One day, Freya's hair was caught in the machinery. She was whirled off the ground, and half her scalp was torn away. It took her four months to recover. The skin was **grafted** back on, but it left a scar. Freya always tried to cover it with her hair or a hat.

Freya often wore a hat to cover a scar on her head.

Developing Skills

Freya was a student at the University of London when World War I broke out in 1914. She immediately left college to train as a nurse. During her training, she caught **typhoid fever** and almost died. Later, although still weak, she worked with an ambulance unit in Italy. After the war, Freya stayed in Italy, living with her mother. Before long, she began to find life dull and unexciting. She wanted to go somewhere with lots of "space, distance, history, and danger." The Arab countries seemed to offer what she wanted, so Freya began to learn Arabic.

"In three years time I could learn enough Persian, Turkish, Kurdish, and Arabic to get about."

To improve her Arabic, Freya went to Syria in 1927. She stayed with a Syrian family so that she could get to know the people well. On this trip, she also went to Jerusalem and Egypt. The more Freya traveled in the Middle East, the more it fascinated her. She decided to learn some languages of the region so that she could move easily throughout the area.

Each year, Freya journeyed farther east, making friends wherever she went. In Baghdad, Iraq, she lived with a shoemaker's family. She then made a long and dangerous journey into **Persia**. She wanted to find the legendary castles where warriors, called Assassins, used to gather. Few Europeans had visited these parts of Persia. In the mountains south of the Caspian Sea, Freya discovered a castle that had never been seen by a European explorer.

Freya spent much of the 1930s in southern Arabia. She loved the landscape. Day after day, she rode by camel across the desert. At night, she camped in the open, gazing up at the stars. At other times, she lived more grandly. She was often a guest of sultans and sheikhs. She became good friends with them and their wives.

As a woman traveler in Arab countries, Freya had a big advantage. She could go where no male traveler had ever been: she could visit the harems. The harem was the part of the house and courtyard where the women lived. No men, except close relatives, were allowed in these protected areas. Freya thus learned a great deal about how both the women and the men of the region lived.

BACKGROUNDER

Many Diseases

Freya had serious illnesses several times in her life. As a result of the typhoid fever she suffered during the war, she became sick easily. She almost died of **malaria** in Persia. For a week, she lay in the open, nursed by a kind stranger whose language she did not understand. Another time, she caught dengue fever. In 1942, when sailing to the United States on a visit, her appendix burst, and she had emergency surgery.

Freya resting in her garden between travels.

BACKGROUNDER

World War II (1939–45)

World War I started when Germany invaded Poland. On one side were the Axis powers, led by Germany, Italy, and Japan. Against them were the Allies, led by Britain, France, the Soviet Union, the United States, and China. The Allies included Canada, Australia, and all other members of the British Empire and Commonwealth.

Accomplishments

Freya raised money for her journeys by writing articles and books about her experiences. She wrote more than twenty books. They were very popular because of her exciting style of writing. By the time World War II broke out in 1939, Freya was well known. She was known not only as a travel writer. She was famous also as an expert on the Arab people and their cultures.

During the war, Freya worked for Britain's Ministry of Information. She served in Aden, Yemen, and Egypt. The British feared that all the Arab countries might join the war on the side of Germany. Freya's job was to see that they did not. One job was to advise the British on how to keep the Arab people friendly. Another job was to persuade the Arabs that it would not be wise to fight the British. That was not an easy task, because some of the Arab countries were under British control. They were longing to get rid of the British so that they could govern their countries independently.

In the 1960s, Freya visited Turkey to research a series of travel books on that country.

Yemen had never been a British **colony**, but it showed signs of being ready to fight on the German side. Freya was determined to prevent this from happening. Secretly, she took a film projector into the country. At that time, many Arabs would not watch films. It was against their religion. Chatting in the harem with the chief minister's wife, Freya told her about the films she had brought. She said she would not dream of showing them without permission. Of course, the minister's wife was eager to see them.

Word soon went around, and before long, many important people had seen Freya's movies. They were official movies about the British navy, the air force, and the army. They made Britain look very strong. As Freya had hoped, Yemen decided not to join the war against the British.

After the war, Freya continued her travels. She went to Afghanistan, Turkey, and other remote places. When she was eighty-seven, she traveled on a pony through the Himalayan mountains. She made friends wherever she went. She was always eager to learn about the countries she visited.

Freya took photographs of the many places she visited.

Quick Notes

- **Freya had a round writing desk. It was on runners so that she could turn it to get at the different drawers and cupboards.**

- **Freya spent the last years of her life in Asolo, Italy. In 1985, the people of Asolo had a big ceremony for her and gave her the keys to the city.**

"I see the horizon. A light blue, a blue band. This is the earth. How beautiful it is!"

Valentina Tereshkova

Soviet Astronaut

Early Years

Valentina often went hungry as a child. Her father had been killed in World War II, and her mother worked in a cotton mill. Her family had very little money. They lived in a small village called Maslennikovo. It was near the Volga River in the Soviet Union. The biggest town nearby was Yaroslavl. That was where Valentina's mother worked and where her brother and sister worked as soon as they were old enough.

Like her brother and sister, Valentina had very little education. Her mother could not afford to send Valentina to school until she was ten. She left when she was seventeen. Her first job was in a tire factory, but she soon joined her mother and sister at the mill. There she learned how to run a huge loom that made linen cloth.

In the evenings, Valentina continued her studies, and like many other young Russians, she joined the Komsomol—the Young Communist League. In her spare time, she took up an unusual sport. She learned to jump by parachute.

The yellow star on the U.S.S.R.'s flag was the symbol of the Communist Party.

BACKGROUNDER

Communism

"Communism" comes from a Latin word that means "belonging to everyone." Under a communist form of government, everything is supposed to be shared by all the people, and everyone is supposed to be equal. In practice, this does not happen. Usually the government controls what people do. The most important people are those who belong to the Communist Party. It is considered a privilege to be allowed to join the party. The first communist country was Russia, in 1917. Five years later, Russia joined with other territories to form the Union of Soviet Socialist Republics (the Soviet Union or U.S.S.R.). In the early 1990s, these republics gave up communism and again became separate countries.

Developing Skills

I n 1959, Valentina joined the Yaroslavl Air Sports Club. There she taught others how to jump by parachute. Meanwhile, she was doing a lot of work for the Komsomol. She did practical work, such as helping new workers find somewhere to live. When Valentina was twenty-three years old, she was elected secretary of the mill's Komsomol, and the following year she applied to join the Communist Party.

One of the most exciting days in Valentina's life was April 12, 1961. That was when Yuri Gagarin, a Soviet astronaut, became the first person to go into space. Valentina gazed up at the sky, wondering what it would be like to circle Earth in a rocket. She always enjoyed looking down on Earth when she was parachute jumping. But to see Earth from space—that would really be something!

Just before joining the training unit, Valentina became a full member of the Communist Party. She was one of the youngest members of the party in the Soviet Union.

Valentina wrote to the Soviet space agency and asked to join the U.S.S.R.'s astronaut program. She told them about her parachute jumping and about her work for the Komsomol. To her delight, they accepted her.

Training at the space center was very tough. It included plenty of hard physical exercise. Valentina had to spend a long time in a chamber of silence, where the force of gravity was increased. This made her feel as if she was being pulled very hard. Another test chamber had the opposite effect. There was no pull of gravity, so she floated around. Everyone was amazed at how well she did. She seemed to be the toughest member of the team.

Valentina also had to do a lot of studying. She learned all about rockets and spaceships. This was difficult for someone who had so little education, but she worked hard. Yuri Gagarin, who helped train her, said that she often studied late at night. In the daytime, she had to learn how to fly a plane.

Valentina did so well in her training that she was given a military rank. She was made a junior lieutenant. By 1963, she was ready to go into space. Her training was complete, and she was about to become the first woman astronaut.

BACKGROUNDER

Why Valentina Was Chosen

There were plenty of women who were more qualified than Valentina. Some were highly educated scientists. Others were skilled pilots. Valentina was neither when she joined the space program. That was one reason why she was chosen. The Soviet premier, Nikita Khrushchev, wanted the first woman in space to be an ordinary worker. Valentina was just the type of person he wanted. She had two things in her favor. She could jump by parachute, and she was a keen member of the Young Communist League.

"She tackled the job stubbornly and devoted much of her own time to study, poring over her books in the evening."
Fellow astronaut
Yuri Gagarin

Valentina took an intensive training course at a space training center near Moscow.

Accomplishments

At 12:30 p.m. on June 16, 1963, Valentina was blasted into space in *Vostok VI*. She was the tenth person in the world to go into space. Like the earlier astronauts, she was making a **solo** flight. Spacecraft could not yet carry more than one person at a time.

Looking down at Earth, Valentina found it even more wonderful than she had dreamed. "I see the horizon. A light blue, a blue band," she said, speaking by radio. "This is the earth. How beautiful it is! Everything is going well."

Valentina stayed in space for three days. By the time she returned to Earth on June 19, she had circled the world forty-eight times, traveling 1.2 million miles (1.9 million kilometers). Even more amazing, she landed before her spaceship. As it cruised over the Soviet Union, she was ejected so that she could land by parachute. She came down near a small village in a remote area. The surprised villagers gave her a big welcome.

Valentina and Yuri Gagarin, the first woman and man in space.

Valentina had an even bigger welcome a few days later. A special ceremony was held in Red Square, Moscow. The nation's leader, Premier Khrushchev, made a speech honoring Valentina. He said that the Soviet Union did not think of women as the "weaker sex." Valentina had proved how strong women really were.

In the following years, Valentina remained very active. She had a busy career in politics and was a member of the Soviet government. She was also involved in various international committees, including the U.S.S.R. Cultural and Friendship Union.

Valentina's public career continued after communism ended and the Soviet Union broke up into different countries. In 1992, she became chairperson of the Russian Association of International Cooperation. Two years later, she became head of the Russian branch of an international scientific and cultural group.

Over the years, Valentina has received many honors. These include Hero of the Soviet Union, the Order of Lenin, and the gold medal of the World Peace Council.

Quick Notes

- **Valentina's father was called Vladimir Tereshkov. According to Russian tradition, Valentina took both these names in a different form. Her full name is Valentina Vladimirovna Tereshkova.**

- **Valentina's friends call her Valya.**

- **Valentina and her husband had one daughter—the first child ever born of parents who had both been in space.**

Valentina's flight lasted 70.8 hours. While orbiting Earth, Valentina sent back a radio message to her mother telling her not to worry.

More Women in Profile

Countless women have been explorers—everything from astronauts to undersea divers. The following pages list a few more women explorers you might want to read about on your own. Use the Suggested Reading list to learn more about these and other women explorers.

1868–1926

Gertrude Bell

English Explorer in the Middle East

Gertrude was one of the most famous explorers in the early years of this century. She traveled throughout the Middle East between 1900 and 1914. During the last few years of her life, Gertrude established an **archeology** museum in Baghdad, Iraq. She insisted that ancient statues and other historic treasures should remain in the country. Until then, anything valuable had been taken and put in European or North American museums.

1867–1922

Nellie Bly

American Journalist and World Traveler

Nellie Bly was the pen-name of Elizabeth Cochrane. She was a reporter for the New York *World* and other newspapers. At a time when most journalists were men, Nellie gained a wide reputation for her honest articles. Nellie would do anything to get a good story. After reading Jules Verne's *Around the World in Eighty Days*, she decided to go

Nellie Bly

around the world in even less time. Carrying one small bag, she set off on November 14, 1889. She returned home on January 25, 1890, exactly 72 days, 6 hours, 10 minutes, and 11 seconds after she set out.

1887–1972

Louise Arner Boyd

American Explorer in the Arctic

Louise first saw the Arctic while on a cruise in 1924. She was fascinated by its splendor. She later led seven expeditions to the Arctic and made some very valuable surveys and charts. A part of Greenland is named Louise Boyd Land in her honor.

1868–1969

Alexandra David-Neel

French Explorer in Asia

In 1910, Alexandra was the first woman to interview the Dalai Lama, the religious leader of Tibet. She was fascinated by Tibet, a country that did not welcome **foreigners**. She studied the **Buddhist** religion and lived for a time with Buddhist nuns. Her most daring feat was to enter the city of Lhasa. This holy city was closed to all foreigners, but in 1924, Alexandra disguised herself as an old Tibetan woman and managed to get in. She lived there for two months without being discovered.

Alexandra David-Neel

1870–1953

Mina Hubbard

Canadian Explorer

In 1905, Mina led an expedition through the wilds of Labrador in northeastern Canada. Her husband had died on an earlier attempt, and Mina was determined to complete the journey for him. With three assistants, she crossed the Labrador peninsula from the North West River to Ungava Bay. During the expedition, Mina made the first accurate map of the river systems of the region. Her book *A Woman's Way through Unknown Labrador* describes her experiences.

1903–41

Amy Johnson

English Pilot

Amy was the first woman to fly **solo** from England to Australia. She had her first flying lesson in 1928, and less than a year later, she received her pilot's license. Amy was still very new to flying when she set off for Australia the following year. She left England on May 5, 1930. She had a rough journey and was forced down by a sandstorm at one point. Even so, she made it to Australia, arriving there on May 24. During World War II, Amy flew for the Air Transport Auxiliary. She disappeared just off the coast of England in 1941. No one ever discovered whether she had been shot down by enemy aircraft or whether she crashed.

1903–1997

Ella Maillart

Swiss Explorer and Journalist

"I had to live in the immensity of Asia, almost at the edge of time and space."

In 1935, Ella made a 3,500-mile (5,600-kilometer) journey through Central Asia, Japan, China, and the Soviet Union. Doing some of the journey on foot, she slept in local inns and village huts, and ate whatever food was available. She later made other difficult journeys. Some of her books include *Turkestan Solo* and *Forbidden Journey*.

1870–1938

Ynes Mexia

Mexican Explorer

"She was the true explorer type and happiest when independent and far from civilization."

Thomas Harper Goodspeed in *Plant Hunters in the Andes*

Ynes's father was Mexican, but she spent her first nine years in Texas. As an adult, she traveled throughout Mexico and South America collecting plants. She discovered more than five hundred new **species**, some of which are named after her. Ynes did not travel in a big group. She preferred to do her exploring alone. On one trip up the Amazon River, she lived with a group of headhunters.

1931–

Dervla Murphy

Irish Traveler and Writer

From the age of ten, when she was given her first bicycle, Dervla wanted to cycle around India. She finally achieved her goal in 1963, when she set off on her first bicycle adventure. After leaving Ireland, Dervla crossed the English Channel and then bicycled to India. On this trip, she spent some time looking after Tibetan refugee children. On another trip, she **trekked** through Ethiopia with a mule. Dervla has since made many other long journeys.

1868–1908

Susie Carson Rijnhart

Canadian Doctor and Traveler

Susie was the second white woman to enter Tibet, a country that did not admit **foreigners** until recently. In 1895, she and her husband, Petrus, quietly slipped into Tibet from China. Once inside, they set up a medical mission, and they made many friends. Hoping to teach Tibetans about Christianity, they later traveled across the mountains toward the holy city of Lhasa. This journey was disastrous. Petrus was killed by robbers, and Susie barely escaped with her life.

1927–88
Sheila Scott
English Pilot

Sheila had a career as an actor and model before she took up flying. She received her pilot's license in 1959 and soon afterwards came fifth in an air race. She was the first person to fly **solo** over the North Pole.

Sheila Scott

1847–1936
May French Sheldon
American Explorer in Africa

Many people thought May French Sheldon mad when she set out to lead an expedition into East Africa in 1891. She went inland as far as Mount Kilimanjaro where the Masai lived. Many people had told her the Masai were to be feared. However, they welcomed her with great ceremony, as did the other people she met. Few of these people had seen a white man, and none had ever seen a white woman. May's guides and porters called her Bebe Bwana ("Lady Boss" in Swahili). When she became sick far inland, they carried her all the way back to the coast. In the early 1900s, she explored parts of West Africa.

1859–1925
Fanny Bullock Workman
American Mountaineer

Fanny arrived in India in 1898 with her husband, William. Although they climbed and explored together, Fanny was always the leader. She had already taken William up mountains in Europe as well as on a bicycle tour of Spain. While bicycling around India, Fanny saw the Himalayas for the first time. She decided to set a record by climbing higher than any other woman. During the next ten years, she climbed several mountains in the Himalayas and reached 23,394 feet (7,130 meters).

Glossary

abolish: to get rid of a law, institution, or custom

archeology: the study of ancient remains

Buddhist: a person who practices Buddhism, a religion followed in many parts of Eastern and Central Asia

colony: a region ruled by a distant country

corset: a tight-fitting undergarment worn by women to shape the body

famine: widespread starvation

foreigner: a person from another country

grafted: when a piece of skin has been moved from one part of a body to another

invalid: a person who is sick for a long period of time

lodestar: a guiding idea

malaria: a fever that is spread by mosquitoes

missionary: a person who goes to another country to preach religion or bring medical help

Persia: a country that included parts of what are now Iran and Afghanistan

plantain: a fruit that is similar to the banana

republic: a country where citizens elect a government whose head is usually a president

Royal Flying Corps: a British group formed in 1912 that trained Canadians and others as war pilots for World War I

runner: a piece on the bottom of something that allows it to move freely

solo: something done without a companion or partner

species: types of plants and animals

suffragette: a woman who works for women's right to vote in elections

summit: the highest point of a mountain

trekked: to travel for a long time under difficult conditions

typhoid fever: a disease often caused by polluted water

witty: clever and amusing

Suggested Reading

Douglas, George M. *Women in the Twenties*. Dallas: Saybrook Publishers, 1986.

Fox, Mary Virginia. *Women Astronauts*. New York: Messner, 1984.

Fraser, Antonia, ed. *Heroes and Heroines*. London: Weiderfeld & Nicolson, 1980.

McLenigan, Valjean. *Women Who Dared*. Austin: Raintree Publishing, 1989.

Middleton, Dorothy. *Victorian Lady Travellers*. London: Routledge & Kegan Paul, 1993.

Olds, Elizabeth. *Women of the Four Winds*. Boston: Houghton Mifflin, 1985.

Raven, Susan and Alison Weir. *Women of Achievement*. New York: Harmony Books, 1981.

Saari, Peggy. *Prominent Women of the 20th Century*. New York: UXL, 1996.

Stefoff, Rebecca. *Women of the World: Women Travelers and Explorers*. New York: Oxford University Press, 1992.

Tinling, Marion. *Women into the Unknown: A Sourcebook on Women Explorers and Travelers*. New York: Greenwood, 1989.

Index

1 2 3 4 5 6 7 8 9 0 Printed in Canada 7 6 5 4 3 2 1 0 9 8